D1551822

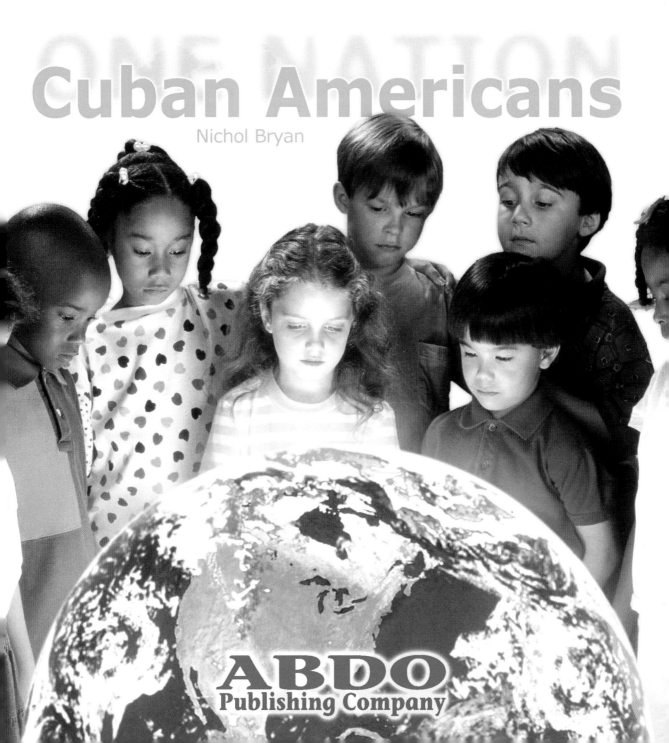

ONE NATION

Cuban Americans

Nichol Bryan

ABDO
Publishing Company

visit us at
www.abdopub.com

Published by ABDO Publishing Company, 4940 Viking Drive, Edina, Minnesota 55435.
Copyright © 2004 by Abdo Consulting Group, Inc. International copyrights reserved in all
countries. No part of this book may be reproduced in any form without written permission from
the publisher.

Printed in the United States.

Cover Photo: Corbis
Interior Photos: AP/Wide World p. 23; Corbis pp. 1, 2-3, 5, 6, 7, 8, 10, 12, 14, 17, 19, 20, 21, 24,
    25, 27, 28, 30-31; Image Direct p. 26; TimePix p. 29

Editors: Kate A. Conley, Jennifer R. Krueger, Kristin Van Cleaf
Art Direction & Maps: Neil Klinepier

All of the U.S. population statistics in the One Nation series are taken from the 2000 Census.

Library of Congress Cataloging-in-Publication Data

Bryan, Nichol, 1958-
    Cuban Americans / Nichol Bryan.
        p. cm. -- (One nation)
    Includes index.
    Summary: Provides information on the history of Cuba and on the customs,
language, religion, and experiences of Cuban Americans.
    ISBN 1-57765-980-5
    1. Cuban Americans--Juvenile literature. [1. Cuban Americans. 2. Immigrants.] I.
Title. II. Series.

E184.C97 B79 2003
973.04687291--dc21

                                                2002043637

Contents

Cuban Americans

Since the 1960s, thousands of Cubans have left their homes for America. When they arrived, they became part of a nation of **immigrants**. In fact, most Americans have ancestors who were born in another country. Today, Cuban Americans continue to make the difficult choice between their homeland and a new world.

Immigrants come to America for different reasons. Some flee the poverty of their own country. Others fear for their safety under **dictators**. Still others come in search of a land that promises endless opportunities. Cubans come to America for the opportunities and freedoms that they are not allowed in Cuba.

Like many immigrants, Cuban Americans face challenges in their new home. They often encounter **discrimination** as they struggle to learn a new language and **culture**. Cuban Americans have succeeded in this new land, although some of them never imagined they would stay. Even as they **thrive** in America, many Cuban Americans still long for the land that was once their home.

A Cuban-American girl studies at a school in Miami's Little Havana.

Cuba's Past

Cuba is an island in the Caribbean Sea. More than 11 million people live on this island, which is about the size of the state of Ohio. Cuba is just 90 miles (145 km) south of Florida. Over the years, many Cubans have made the voyage to Florida. Why have so many Cubans left their island? The answer lies in Cuba's history.

Christopher Columbus, an Italian explorer, visited the island in 1492. He was on a journey of exploration for the country of Spain. Spain's king and queen, Ferdinand II and Isabella I, paid for his voyage.

Spain turned Cuba into a colony. Most of the native people died under the harsh treatment of the Spaniards. Later, the Spaniards brought African slaves to Cuba to grow **sugarcane** and other crops.

Christopher Columbus

Cuba gained independence in 1898, after the **Spanish-American War**. For the first years after independence, Cuba was ruled by a series of governments that cared little for the people. In the 1930s, Fulgencio Batista seized control of the country. He became a cruel and **corrupt dictator**.

In 1959, Fidel Castro led a revolution that forced Batista out of power. Castro promised a better life for Cubans. He provided more land for people with small farms. He started social programs to help the poor. Castro's rule, however, was often harsh. He had his political enemies killed or put in prison. He did not allow his opponents to speak out.

Fulgencio Batista

For these reasons, thousands of people left Cuba during Castro's first few years in power. Some were **corrupt** officials from Batista's government. Others were wealthy people who lost their land or businesses after the revolution. Some were ordinary people who feared what Castro might do. They fled to the United States and elsewhere.

Officials in the U.S. government worried that Castro was a **communist**. They wanted him out of power. So, U.S. officials secretly organized 1,400 Cuban Americans to invade Cuba in 1961.

Castro being sworn in as the ruler of Cuba in 1959

They thought that once the invasion started, Cubans would rise up and overthrow Castro. However, the invasion failed. It became known as the Bay of Pigs invasion.

The United States also launched an **economic** embargo of Cuba. That meant Cuba could not sell goods to the United States. It also meant Cuba could not buy the goods it needed from the United States. The embargo hurt Cuba's economy. People got poorer and poorer.

As time went on, Castro's government clamped down harder on the people. Few political freedoms were allowed. It became more difficult for Cubans to leave the country. So, some tried to sail from Cuba to Florida to escape.

However, this voyage is a difficult one. Some people drowned. Others ran into bad weather. Still others were chased down by the Cuban navy. Many of these **refugees** did not succeed in reaching Florida.

Since Castro took power in 1959, millions of people have tried to leave Cuba. The United States has promised to accept 20,000 Cuban refugees every year. This means the government must send some refugees back to Cuba. Despite this, thousands of Cubans risk their lives every year to live in America.

The Voyage

Take a minute to find Cuba on a map. It doesn't look far from Florida, does it? Under ideal conditions, and with a safe boat, the trip can be made almost overnight. But, many Cubans have lost their lives trying to survive this short voyage. There are many reasons for this.

Cuban refugees on their voyage to the United States

Often, Cubans make their escape in unsafe boats. These boats may leak, may not have a motor, or may be too small for the ocean. However, this doesn't stop many Cubans from making the journey. In fact, if someone hears that a neighbor is going to sneak away, often many other people want to go, too. So, sometimes the boats are overcrowded, which makes them tip easily.

In addition, bad weather can make a boat trip even more dangerous. Summer and fall are **hurricane** seasons. No one wants to be on the ocean when these storms hit. And, if a boat does not have a motor or good sails, it may take days to reach land. Some **refugees** have run out of food and water on this voyage.

The Journey from Cuba to the United States

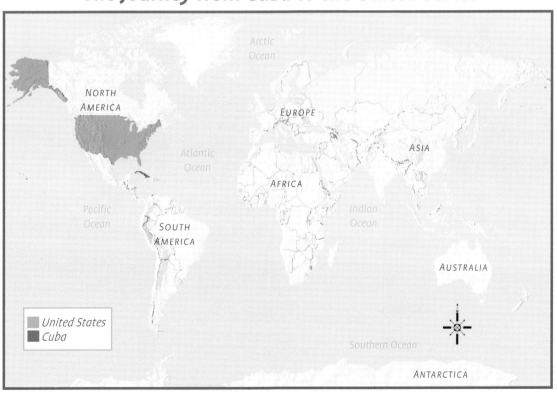

Elián González

Ships from both the United States and Cuba are on the lookout for these boats. Sailors in the U.S. Coast Guard sometimes pick up people seeking protection in the United States. But, to discourage **refugees** from risking their lives, the United States sends most Cubans found at sea back to Cuba. Those who reach the United States may or may not be allowed to stay.

Refugees who are returned to Cuba face problems. They may be jailed for trying to escape. Moreover, their neighbors may reject them. Cuban Americans usually feel that these refugees should be allowed to stay in the United States and become citizens.

Cuban Americans felt especially strong about the fate of Elián González. In 1999, Elián's mother tried to escape Cuba with Elián when he was five years old. His mother died during the boat trip. A fisher saved Elián from death in the Caribbean Sea before taking him to U.S. Coast Guard sailors.

Elián was brought to relatives in Florida. But his father, who lived in Cuba, wanted Elián with him. The boy's relatives in the United States did not want to give him up. In the end, the U.S. government decided Elián belonged with his father and sent him back to Cuba.

For many, separating from their families is the hardest part about leaving Cuba. Once a Cuban leaves the island, it is not easy to return. Some Cuban Americans have not seen their children or grandchildren for years. Cuban Americans often send money, medicine, food, and other items to their relatives in Cuba.

Life in America

Today, more than 1.2 million Cuban Americans live in the United States. The largest communities are in southern Florida. Smaller groups live mostly along the U.S. East Coast, in states such as New Jersey.

Starting over in America has been harder for some Cuban Americans than for others. The first Cubans to come to the United States in the 1960s were usually well educated and wealthy. These Cubans had an easier time fitting into American society than have other Cuban **immigrants**.

This hairstylist works in one of Little Havana's many small businesses.

More recent Cuban immigrants usually come from a lower social class in Cuba than the first Cuban immigrants. So, sometimes they have a harder time finding acceptance in America, even in the Cuban-American community.

As Cuban Americans work to succeed in America, many struggle with the memory of their homeland. Many feel that Cuba is still their home. Even Cuban Americans who were born in the United States sometimes feel that they really belong in Cuba.

Cuban-American Communities

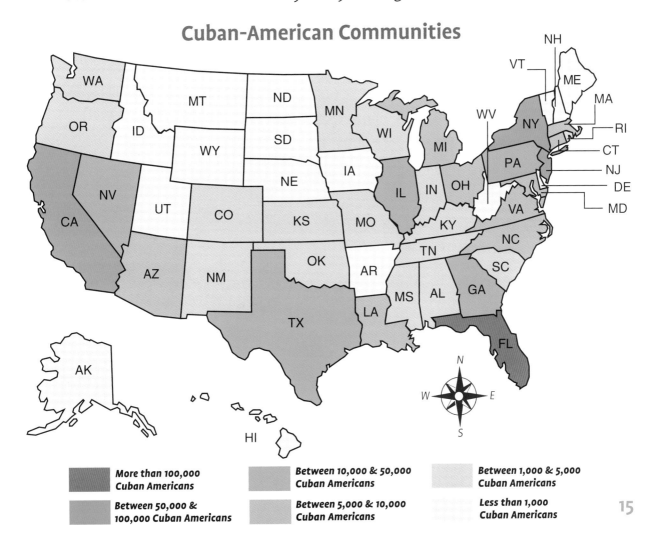

| | More than 100,000 Cuban Americans | | Between 10,000 & 50,000 Cuban Americans | | Between 1,000 & 5,000 Cuban Americans |
| | Between 50,000 & 100,000 Cuban Americans | | Between 5,000 & 10,000 Cuban Americans | | Less than 1,000 Cuban Americans |

Becoming a Citizen

Cubans and other **immigrants** who come to the United States take the same path to citizenship. Immigrants become citizens in a process called naturalization. A government agency called the Immigration and Naturalization Service (INS) oversees this process.

The Path to Citizenship

Applying for Citizenship

The first step in becoming a citizen is filling out a form. It is called the Application for Naturalization. On the application, immigrants provide information about their past. Immigrants send the application to the INS.

Providing Information

Besides the application, immigrants must provide the INS with other items. They may include documents such as marriage licenses or old tax returns. Immigrants must also provide photographs and fingerprints. They are used for identification. The fingerprints are also used to check whether immigrants have committed crimes in the past.

The Interview

Next, an INS officer interviews each immigrant to discuss his or her application and background. In addition, the INS officer tests the immigrant's ability to speak, read, and write in English. The officer also tests the immigrant's knowledge of American civics.

The Oath

Immigrants approved for citizenship must take the Oath of Allegiance. Once immigrants take this oath, they are citizens. During the oath, immigrants promise to renounce loyalty to their native country, to support the U.S. Constitution, and to serve and defend the United States when needed.

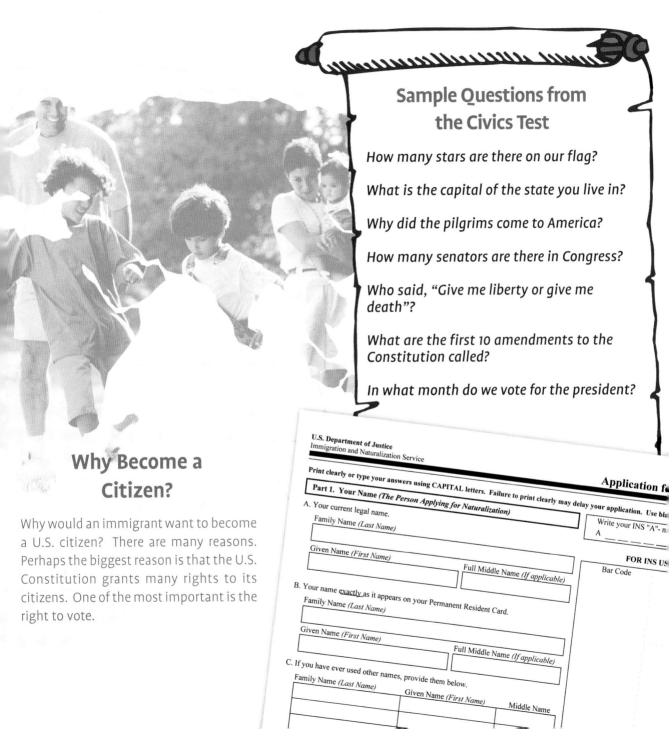

Sample Questions from the Civics Test

How many stars are there on our flag?

What is the capital of the state you live in?

Why did the pilgrims come to America?

How many senators are there in Congress?

Who said, "Give me liberty or give me death"?

What are the first 10 amendments to the Constitution called?

In what month do we vote for the president?

Why Become a Citizen?

Why would an immigrant want to become a U.S. citizen? There are many reasons. Perhaps the biggest reason is that the U.S. Constitution grants many rights to its citizens. One of the most important is the right to vote.

U.S. Department of Justice
Immigration and Naturalization Service

Print clearly or type your answers using CAPITAL letters. Failure to print clearly may delay your application. Use bla

Application f

Part 1. Your Name *(The Person Applying for Naturalization)*

A. Your current legal name.

Family Name *(Last Name)*

Given Name *(First Name)*

Full Middle Name *(If applicable)*

Write your INS "A"- n

A _ _ _ _ _ _

FOR INS US

Bar Code

B. Your name <u>exactly</u> as it appears on your Permanent Resident Card.

Family Name *(Last Name)*

Given Name *(First Name)*

Full Middle Name *(If applicable)*

C. If you have ever used other names, provide them below.

Family Name *(Last Name)*

Given Name *(First Name)*

Middle Name

A Cultural Mix

Cuban **immigrants** have brought their **culture** to the United States. Cuban culture is a mix of Spanish and African traditions. Over time, Cuban Americans have held on to their culture while adapting to their new homeland. This can be seen in Cuban-American families. It is also present in Cuban-American music, food, religion, and language.

Family

Cubans place a lot of importance on family. In Cuba, people often live in large families. Sometimes grandparents, uncles, and aunts all live in the same home. Traditionally, the father in a Cuban family has all the power outside the home. The mother, however, is responsible for doing the work inside the home.

Opposite page: A family eats at a restaurant in Little Havana.

In the United States, Cuban Americans still have strong family ties. But, the roles of fathers and mothers have become less traditional. In fact, many Cuban-American women have become business and political leaders.

A Musical Tradition

One of the best-known parts of Cuban culture is its music. Cuba's rumba, mambo, and cha-cha blend lively Spanish-inspired tunes with driving African rhythms. Cuban Americans have brought this music to the United States, where it has become popular with other Americans, too.

Dancers perform during a parade celebrating Cuban culture in Miami.

A fruit stand in a Cuban-American neighborhood

Food

Cuban Americans have also brought special dishes to the United States. They have the spice and flavors of Hispanic and African foods. Black beans and rice is a typical Cuban meal. Cuban Americans may also fry bananas or boil **yucca** for a traditional dish. They often cook using garlic **marinades** and roasted meat.

Religion

Most Cuban Americans are Roman Catholic. Spaniards brought this religion to Cuba. However, in Castro's Cuba, religion was not encouraged. Many Cubans stopped practicing their religion. But, some want to keep a link to their traditional faith. Others see being Catholic as a way of showing they dislike what Castro has done to Cuba.

Catholics honor many saints. Our Lady of Charity of Cobre is an important saint to Catholic Cubans. According to legend, two Cuban fishers survived a terrible storm at sea. Afterward, they found a mysterious statue of the **Virgin Mary** floating in the water. The fishers believed she saved their lives. The people built a shrine to the statue and named her Our Lady of Charity. In 1916, Pope Benedict XV named her the special protector of Cuba.

Some Cuban Americans practice a religion called Santeria. It grew from the traditions of African slaves in Cuba. Santeria blends parts of Christian and West African beliefs. Santerians believe in one God, but also in saints or spirits known as *orishas*. They believe *orishas* can help people on Earth, just as Catholic saints can.

Santerians also believe that rituals involving music and offerings of food and animal sacrifice to the spirits can help people find solutions to their problems. A growing number of Cubans in the United States practice Santeria. However, many Catholic priests and other Cuban Americans disapprove of Santeria.

Believers in Santeria practice their religion at a church in Florida.

Language

Many Cuban Americans speak Spanish. Cuban Spanish is similar to that spoken by other Hispanics. However, there are a few differences. For instance, some Cubans don't pronounce the letter *s* at the end of some words. Cuban Spanish also includes some words from African languages. These include *asere*, which means "buddy," and *iriampo*, which is slang for "food."

*Signs in Spanish are common in Little Havana. This main street is known as **Calle Ocho**.*

Some new Cuban Americans face an odd problem when it comes to language. It is difficult for those who live around Miami, Florida, to learn English. That's because they are not around anyone who routinely speaks it! If they work in a Cuban area of Miami called Little Havana, they may not hear a word of English from dawn to dusk.

A customer in Little Havana orders from a menu written in Spanish.

Cuban Fame

America has always had a special love for Cuban **culture**. The excitement, color, and rhythm of Cuba have appealed to thousands of Americans. Not surprisingly, many Cuban entertainers have found fame in America.

One of the first Cuban-American stars was Desi Arnaz. He was a singer and the leader of a Cuban band. Arnaz was also a television actor. In the 1950s, he starred with his wife, Lucille Ball, in the hit television show *I Love Lucy*. Arnaz introduced millions of Americans to Cuban music on the show.

Gloria Estefan wears a T-shirt that reads Cuba B.C., or Cuba Before Castro.

Arnaz also paved the way for more recent Cuban-American stars. One of them is singer Gloria Estefan. She won a Grammy Award for her album *Mi Tierra* in 1993, and for *Abriendo Puertas* in 1995. She won another Grammy Award in 2001 for her album *Alma Caribeña*. Each of these albums is in Spanish. Estefan has also spoken on behalf of Cuban Americans who oppose Fidel Castro.

Another Cuban-American star is Andy Garcia. He was born in Cuba and came to America with his family when he was five years old. Garcia has starred in many hit movies, including *Ocean's Eleven* and *When a Man Loves a Woman*. He now owns a film production company called CineSon Productions.

Andy Garcia on the set of The Godfather: Part III

Baseball is another area where Cuban Americans have made an impact on the United States. Cuban-American slugger Jose Canseco had a great career with the Oakland Athletics and other teams. Orlando Hernandez is a dazzling pitcher with the New York Yankees. And, Tony Perez helped the Cincinnati Reds win the World Series. He was inducted into the American Baseball Hall of Fame in 2000.

Cuban Americans have also contributed to the arts in the United States. Mario Sanchez is a renowned painter. He was born to Cuban parents in Key West, Florida. He taught himself how to paint and sculpt. His **folk-art** paintings of life in the Florida Keys are popular with collectors.

Jose Canseco

Oscar Hijuelos has also contributed to the arts. He is a Cuban-American author who has written award-winning novels. In books such as *The Mambo Kings Play Songs of Love*, Hijuelos writes about the lives of

Oscar Hijuelos

Cubans who came to the United States. The people in his books try to succeed in America but always remember their lives in Cuba.

Cuban Americans are proud of their accomplishments. But, their future is always uncertain. Many wonder what will happen to Cuba when Castro's rule ends. Some Cuban Americans hope to return to their homeland one day. However, many may discover that they are now more American than Cuban.

Glossary

communist - a person who supports communism. It is a social and economic system in which everything is owned by the government and distributed to the people as needed.

corrupt - showing dishonest or improper behavior.

culture - the customs, arts, and tools of a nation or people at a certain time.

dictator - a ruler with complete control who usually governs in a cruel or unfair way.

discrimination - unfair treatment based on factors such as a person's race, religion, or gender.

economy - the way a nation uses its money, goods, and natural resources.

folk art - art made by people with no formal training. It usually shows scenes from everyday life.

hurricane - a tropical storm with strong circular winds, rain, thunder, and lightning.

immigration - entry into another country to live. People who immigrate are called immigrants.

marinade - a liquid that moistens and flavors meat or vegetables before cooking.

refugee - a person who flees to another country for safety and protection.

Spanish-American War (1898) - a war between the United States and Spain that ended Spanish rule of Cuba and other colonies.

sugarcane - a tall grass with a thick stem from which sugar is produced.

thrive - to prosper.

Virgin Mary - the mother of Jesus.

yucca - a group of plants with white flowers found in Latin America and the United States.

Saying It

Abriendo Puertas - ah-bree-EN-do PUER-tahs
Alma Caribeña - AHL-mah kahr-ee-BEH-nya
Cobre - KOH-bray
Elián González - el-YAHN gohn-ZAH-lehs
Fidel Castro - fee-DEL KAS-troh
Fulgencio Batista - fool-HEN-see-oh bah-TEES-tah
Mi Tierra - ME tee-EHR-ah
orishas - OH-ree-shahs
Oscar Hijuelos - OHS-kahr ee-HWAY-lohs
Santaria - san-tuh-REE-uh

Web Sites

To learn more about Cuban Americans, visit ABDO Publishing Company on the World Wide Web at **www.abdopub.com**. Web sites about Cuban Americans are featured on our Book Links page. These links are routinely monitored and updated to provide the most current information available.

31

Index